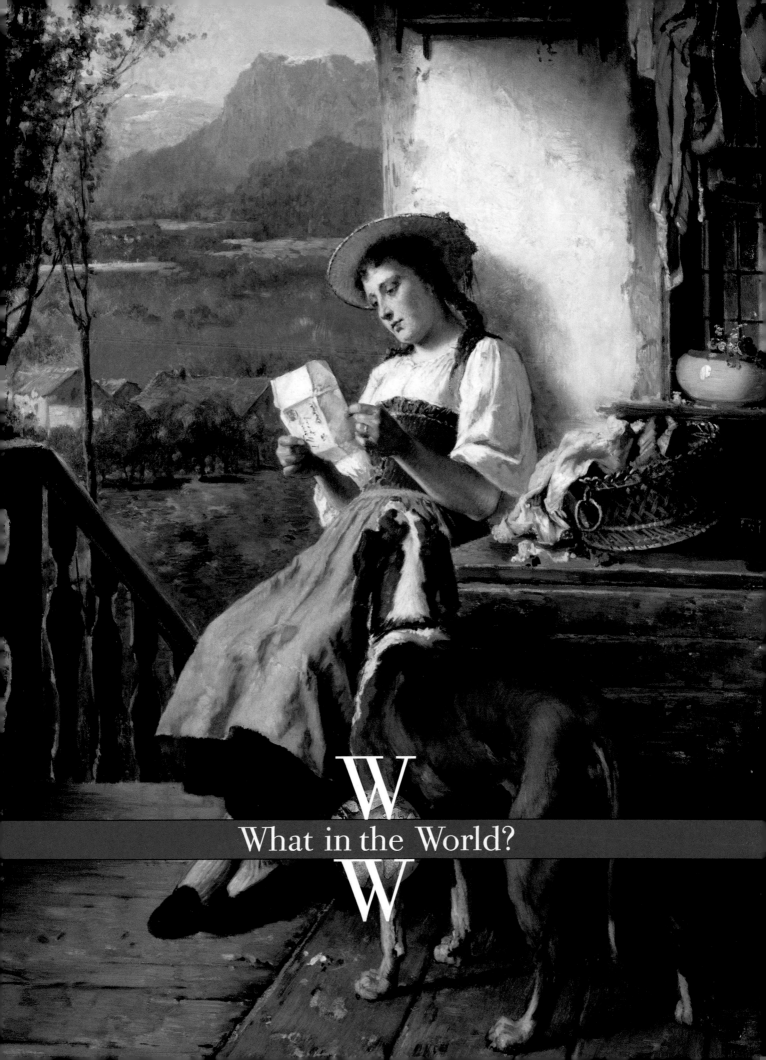

W
W
What in the World?

The Postage Stamp

Jennifer Fandel

What in the World?

Creative Education
an imprint of The Creative Company

Never before had a face accomplished so much. Adorning the world's first postage stamp, her face crisscrossed England and eventually traveled to the ends of the British Empire, bringing news to those separated by oceans, mountains, and deserts. Set in simple profile against an inky black background, the face of Victoria—

In 1837, 18-year-old Queen Victoria began her 64-year reign. London's Buckingham Palace, completed the year before by British architect John Nash, became her royal residence.

Britain's new, young queen—was smooth as a statue and serious with the mission of leading the most powerful nation in the world. Her subjects fell in love with her image and the affordable means of communication that it represented. Costing only a penny, the postage stamp finally put letters into everyone's hands.

Postage stamps enabled people to send letters all over the world.

The 1840 stamp that bears the image of a youthful Queen Victoria is now worth around $3,000.

The first railroad to span the United States was completed in 1869.

Egypt's first steam locomotive was used in 1852 to power passenger trains.

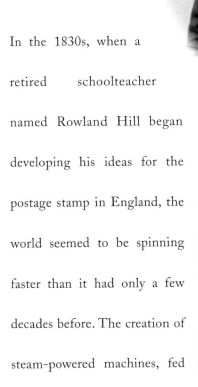

In the 1830s, when a retired schoolteacher named Rowland Hill began developing his ideas for the postage stamp in England, the world seemed to be spinning faster than it had only a few decades before. The creation of steam-powered machines, fed by coal, led to rapid industrialization throughout all of Great Britain. In turn, cities—blackened from the constant belching of coal dust—boomed as job seekers poured in from the English countryside. Opportunists left their family and friends back home, sometimes never seeing or hearing from them again.

Rowland Hill liked to invent in his spare time. In 1826, he described in his journal a traveling post office, which would allow mail to be sorted on the way to its destination.

England's Industrial Revolution created a rising middle class that Rowland Hill (above) wanted to educate.

Ships carried Victorian explorers to new lands and brought written communication home again.

The British Empire encompassed territories on all continents and brought industrialization and rapid transportation to each. The United States, Russia, and European countries also began laying track for steam-powered trains, and, after the first transatlantic steamship crossings in 1838, people were able to satisfy their desire for movement.

Explorers cut swaths through unknown territories from South America to Africa, penning accounts in their journals and drawing maps for places outsiders had once only imagined. Yet, without a reliable method by which to send this information back home, observations of adventurers and travelers remained private, unable to be shared.

Simeon Denis Poisson (opposite) published more than 300 works related to mathematics and science.

In 1837, French mathematician Simeon Denis Poisson established early theories on probability. He based his theories on a rare occurrence—the number of deaths in the French army due to mule kicks.

Mount Holyoke Female Seminary, the first college in the United States exclusively for women, was founded by Mary Lyon in 1837. At the time, there were 120 U.S. colleges for men and none for women.

In 1837, Tiffany and Co. was founded in New York. The store, now known for its fine jewelry and luxury goods, started as a stationery and fancy goods store. The first Tiffany jewelry was created in 1848.

To the south of England, in central Africa, communication remained the same as it had for centuries, as people relied on word of mouth to disseminate information. European demand for goods such as ivory, wax, and rubber helped isolated tribes gain recognition and flourish through trade. Information was also exchanged with Arab-Swahili traders from East Africa, who developed new routes and partnerships with their central African neighbors.

In Australia, the native Aborigines also continued to pass on information within their communities through drawings on rock walls. These drawings, known as "X-ray drawings" for their portrayal of both the outsides and insides of animals and people, went unnoticed by the British settlers rapidly populating the land, who largely disregarded the nomadic people and what they considered to be their primitive ways.

For the Aborigines, painting was a sacred act, but they also used drawings (opposite) to tell stories.

Many countries developed stamps that showed familiar images, such as these Chinese boats.

In 1837, German archaeologist Georg Friedrich Grotefend deciphered Persian cuneiform, a type of wedge-shaped writing, dating from 3,000 B.C. His work would increase knowledge about Middle Eastern cultures.

China, known for an ancient civilization that had developed paper in the second century A.D. and an extensive postal service three centuries earlier, turned back to artistic forms of communication in the early 1800s. Artists looked to archaic writings found on seals, stones, and earthenware vessels to develop a new style of calligraphy. This beautiful style of writing, an art form in itself, involved its readers emotionally.

Across the Pacific, the South American country of Brazil gained independence from Portugal in 1822 and crowned Pedro I emperor. His son, Dom Pedro II, became the second (and last) emperor of Brazil in 1840. Dom Pedro was known for his support of education and the arts, and also endorsed the new and intriguing art form of photography. In its infancy at the time, photography had the ability to do what no other art had done: communicate an experience exactly as one saw it.

Dom Pedro II (opposite) ruled Brazil for 49 years and abolished slavery in that country.

Nineteenth-century intellectuals Henry David Thoreau (left) and Ralph Waldo Emerson (right).

In the U.S., an emphasis on rugged individualism, self-reliance, and a return to nature came to life in New England. The Transcendentalists, whose proponents included such famed American writers as Ralph Waldo Emerson and Henry David Thoreau, began their progressive social movement with discussions of philosophy and religion. Those involved in the movement believed that individual intuition was the highest form of knowledge a person could possess.

Scottish blacksmith Kirkpatrick Macmillan invented the modern bicycle in 1839, complete with a pedal system and brake. The bike weighed 57 pounds (26 kg).

*The first electric telegraph (above) was invented in 1831;
a later copy of Kirkpatrick Macmillan's 1839 bicycle (below).*

In 1843, Samuel Morse built the world's first long-distance telegraph line between Washington, D.C., and Baltimore, Maryland. The following year, he transmitted his first message from the Capitol: "What hath God wrought?"

The centennial of America's national pastime was commemorated in 1939 with a special three-cent stamp.

Abner Doubleday's vision of the game of baseball came alive when Doubleday Field was built in Cooperstown, New York.

In 1839, a young West Point cadet from New York named Abner Doubleday devised the rules for the game of baseball. It would be played on a diamond-shaped field with two teams of nine players.

To ward off hunger between lunch and dinner, the British Duchess of Bedford, Anna, introduced the practice of afternoon tea in 1840. At the time, the British drank more coffee than tea.

Afternoon tea consisted of a light meal of sandwiches or scones.

As travel took people farther away from one another, they needed a new means of communication to keep in touch. In the early 1800s, writing a letter was much like putting a message into a bottle and sending it out to sea; it was a gamble whether anyone would ever read it or not. Rowland Hill, a systematic British man, saw the world for its potential to share information and sought to put that message into the correct hands.

In 1795, Rowland Hill was born in Kidderminster, an English town close to the industrial city of Birmingham. The third son of a schoolmaster, Rowland was a creative, studious, and self-motivated child. In love with numbers at an early age, he spent much of his

New Zealand was made a British colony in 1841. Settlers cut millions of acres of forest for sheep pasture, causing wide-spread land erosion and ill will between settlers and Maori natives.

time counting and calculating when a bout of scarlet fever at age four kept him in bed for months. His parents encouraged his fasci-nations, and his father, interested in building and inventing, gave his sons free rein with his tools and the school's blacksmith forge.

Learning basic arithmetic was a fundamental part of a 19th-century child's education.

Many countries utilized images of important people—such as monarchs—on their stamps.

Christmas cards typically feature familiar figures such as Santa Claus.

While Rowland began his formal education at age seven, he had already discovered that much learning came from careful study of the world around him. After school each day, he did chores and, by age eight, was selling crops from his own garden plot, using the money to buy books. Inspired by stories of noble characters who performed memorable deeds, Rowland set high standards for himself and others, especially regarding efficiency and punctuality. He implemented a system at school to make the period bells ring at regular intervals, and at home, he encouraged his mother to plan her meals so that they would be served at regular times. When he was only 14, Rowland began doing the accounting at his father's school, and two years later, he was managing his father's accounts in full.

Rowland's philosophy of education did not involve using humiliating punishments such as the dunce cap.

The propagation of knowledge was especially important to Rowland. As a teenager, he worked as his father's teaching assistant and later managed a school with his older brother Matthew in Birmingham. His brother focused on improving teaching methods, while Rowland managed the school's organization and finances. In 1818, Rowland and his brother wrote an educational primer, *Plans for the Government and Education of Boys in Large Numbers*, which was published in 1822. In 1826, 31-year-old Rowland founded his own school for boys in the Tottenham region of London, moving there with his wife, Caroline, a childhood friend. In his school, Hill broke from the traditional system of physical punishment and instead encouraged his pupils with rewards.

The great auk, a flightless bird similar to the penguin, became extinct in 1844. The birds nested on rocky islands off Iceland, Greenland, and Newfoundland and were killed for their flesh and feathers.

In 1841, English entrepreneur Samuel Shepheard opened the Hotel des Anglais in Cairo, Egypt. It was the last British outpost between Gibraltar and India where people could pick up mail and hold international meetings.

Now found only in illustrations, great auks used their wings to swim underwater.

South Africa has long been one of the largest exporters of fruit in the world.

Travelers along the historic Oregon Trail often rode in covered wagons.

In 1847, around 2,000 pioneers followed the Oregon Trail to Utah.

U.S. Army Lieutenant John Charles Fremont and his guide Kit Carson mapped the route for the Oregon Trail in 1842. That same year, a wagon train of 120 people initiated large-scale immigration to the Oregon Territory.

In 1833, Rowland retired from teaching and began a career with the British government, becoming involved in campaigns to colonize South Australia. This led to his appointment as secretary to the South Australian colonization commission in 1835. Rowland also worked to improve education through the distribution of literature. He first tried to abolish the stamp tax on newspapers, hoping that this would encourage more publishing and more reading. But it was a chance encounter on the street one day in 1836 that led to Rowland's most famous work.

Unlike the rest of the country, South Australia was not colonized by convicts but by free settlers.

Belgian painter Charles Baugniet shows a woman engaged in a common 19th-century activity in The Letter.

In 1974, self-adhesive stamps were introduced in the U.S. but were unpopular. Reintroduced in 1994, they now account for the majority of stamps produced.

While he was out walking, Rowland witnessed a peasant girl refusing a letter. At the time, the postal service was slow and unreliable, and the recipients of letters paid the postage when—or if—they received their mail. Rowland hadn't realized, though, that the high costs of postage deterred many from accepting their mail. It cost more than a day's pay for the average worker to send mail 300 miles (483 km), from London to Scotland. To mail a letter overseas, the cost was more than a week's wages. Believing that lower postage rates would help the education of the nation, as people of all classes would be able to share their ideas and opinions cheaply and openly, Rowland began an investigation into the British postal system.

In 1920, Americans could send certain letters for only two cents.

In January 1837, Rowland put forth a radical suggestion in his pamphlet *Post Office Reform: Its Importance and Practicality*, which he presented to the government. He called for a uniform rate of one penny with the sender paying postage, indicated by attaching postal labels on the letter with paste.

His proposal met with harsh criticism. Post office officials feared that reducing postage from 12 pence to a penny would mean that 12 times as much mail would need to be sent to break even, requiring 12 times as much work. Most members of Parliament also opposed Rowland's plan because he wanted to end free postal services for the government. Postmaster General Lord Lichfield summed up their opinions, stating: "With respect to the plan set forth by Mr. Hill, of all the wild and visionary schemes which I have ever heard or read, it is the most extravagant."

On the Italian island of Sardinia in the early 1800s, people stamped their stationery with different values, according to distance. This was not a postal fee but a tax on privately carried letters.

Some claim that Scottish printer James Chalmers invented the postage stamp. In 1834, he designed round, adhesive stamps for postage, but they remained buried in his desk until he heard about Hill's postage proposal.

With cheap stamps, anyone, after putting pen to paper, could send a letter to anywhere in the world.

In the 19th century, letters were written using a straight pen with a nib that was dipped into an inkwell.

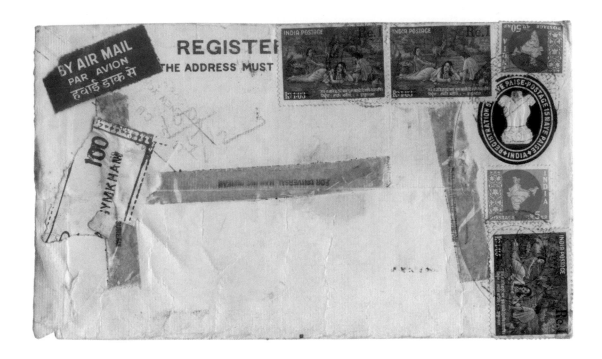

Multiple stamps are often necessary to pay for postage to faraway places.

Yet, in the fall of 1837, Parliament formed a postage committee. Committee members, businessmen, lawyers, and tradespeople put enough pressure on the government that Rowland's ideas spun into action. In 1839, the British Postal Reform Act was passed, approving the reduction of postage to a penny, and over the next year, a miniature portrait put more letters into people's hands than ever before.

The Penny Black was designed without the country of origin specified. British stamps still do not specify where they are from, but they do incorporate the image of the reigning monarch.

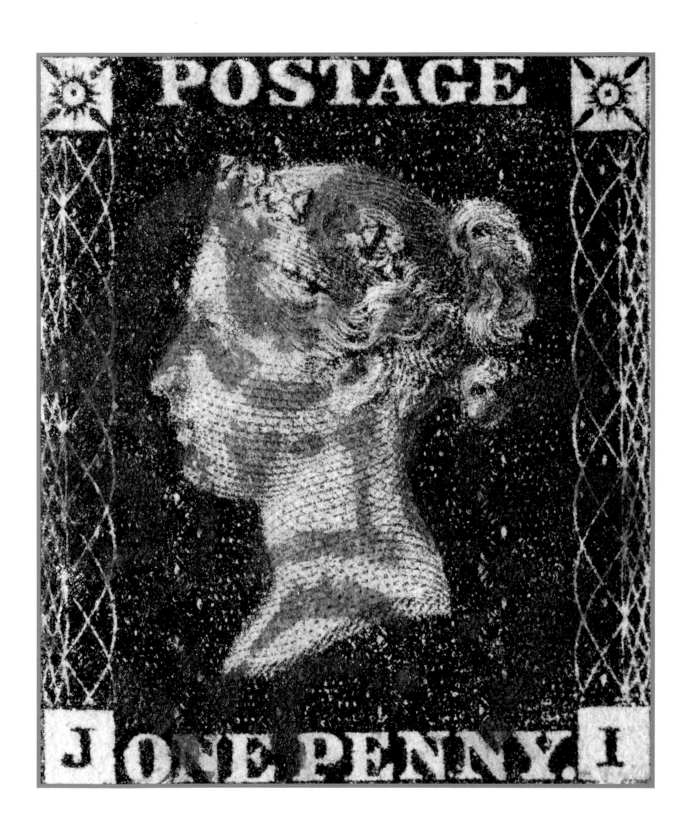

The Penny Black, the world's first postage stamp.

UNITED STATES POSTAGE

A Stamp on the World

In 1839, out of a piece of bright, polished steel, a miniature face emerged in a delicate frame. Months before, the British treasury department had held a contest for the design of the world's first postage stamp and chose, out of more than 2,600 entries, a stamp of a woman's face. Hill and those in the treasury were especially taken with the artist's notion that fraud—a serious concern with this new postal money—would be more recognizable in a face,

From 1838 to 1839, more than 15,000 Cherokee Indians traveled 800 miles (1,288 km) on the "Trail of Tears." About 4,000 people died on the journey from their southeastern homes to reservations in the western U.S.

rather than in a decorative design.

The artist's stamp of a woman's face reminded Hill of artist William Wyon's medal of 18-year-old Queen Victoria, commissioned when she became Britain's reigning monarch in 1837. That face, Hill believed, was the image for the stamps. Once the final designs, called essays, were approved, famed engraver Charles Heath began the meticulous job of engraving the printing die for the stamp.

In 1959, the U.S. Postal Service marked President Abraham Lincoln's 150th birthday with a one-cent stamp.

Into softened steel, Heath carved the head of the queen. He worked on the eye alone for five days, and the whole rectangular picture—measuring only 7/8 by 3/4 inches (2.22 by 1.9 cm)—took several weeks to complete. The stamps would be printed using a technique called intaglio, in which incisions in the engraving absorb the ink. On the image of the queen, he carved fine lines to highlight her features and the curls of her hair. For the dark background, he made crisscrossed grooves that would absorb the ink.

The first triangular stamps were issued in 1853 at the Cape of Good Hope in South Africa to help illiterate postal clerks distinguish between their postage and the rectangular postage of other countries.

Prepaid letter sheets and envelopes called "Mulreadys" made their debut at the same time as the Penny Blacks. The stationery, which bore images of the postal service improving people's lives, was ridiculed by the public.

South Africa introduced triangular stamps, but other countries such as Spain have long used them, too.

Today, a judge for an artistic stamp contest has many options to consider before choosing the winning design.

In 1837, English pharmacists John Wheeley Lea and William Perrins introduced Lea & Perrins Worcestershire Sauce. The sauce, which still exists today, originally followed a recipe by Lord Sandys, the former governor of Bengal in India.

Hill chose black ink for the first one-penny stamps, and printing presses produced 50,000 "Penny Blacks" (so named for their value and color) a day. At the same time, smaller batches of the "Twopenny Blue" were produced, as the postal service correctly estimated that few people would send mail heavier than half an ounce (14.2 g). After printing, an adhesive made from potato starch, wheat starch, and gum was added to the sheets. Each stamp had to be cut from the rest of the sheet with a scissors or knife.

A stamp celebrating the U.S. Postal Service's first 100 years incorporated the subjects from the original 1847 stamps.

On May 1, 1840, the world's first postage stamps went on sale in England, and people rushed to post offices to buy their very own image of the queen at a price that was little more than a loaf of bread. Throughout that year, people sent twice as many letters as they had the year before, and the printing presses ran night and day to keep up with the demand. Between May 1840 and January 1841, 72 million Penny Blacks were sold.

In 1843, Brazil and Switzerland followed Britain in the issue of stamps. In 1847, the first U.S. postage stamps were sold. Ben Franklin's image adorned the five-cent stamp, and George Washington appeared on the 10-cent stamp.

Since 1855, British people have posted mail in freestanding pillar boxes.

This 16th-century lady had to depend upon her maid to deliver her love letters.

During the mid-1600s, stamped seals were used in Paris, and letterboxes were placed on all main streets. This system was devised to help France's teenage king, Louis XIV, communicate with his love interests.

In the 1890s, Canada, Newfoundland, and New Zealand were allowed a stamp of the English queen in her later years, so that her more remote subjects could see what she looked like.

While the image on the postage stamp itself fascinated the British public, they were even more taken with the now affordable, reliable, and private method of communication open to them. Although the Penny Black and Twopenny Blue were created by the government, many regarded them as stamps of independence, since individuals could send mail without interference from the government. In the past, once mail left the sender, it belonged to the government post office until it was paid for and delivered. Postal officials could open mail if they desired, and spies occasionally worked for the post office to gather information. But the new postage stamps were a symbolic government guarantee that people's right to privacy would not be infringed upon.

A Swiss stamp (above); Switzerland's postal service was also created by the government but is now an independent company.

Throughout much of the British Empire, beginning in the late 1700s, adhesive labels were used to indicate tax paid on specific goods such as hats, wallpaper, and even newspapers.

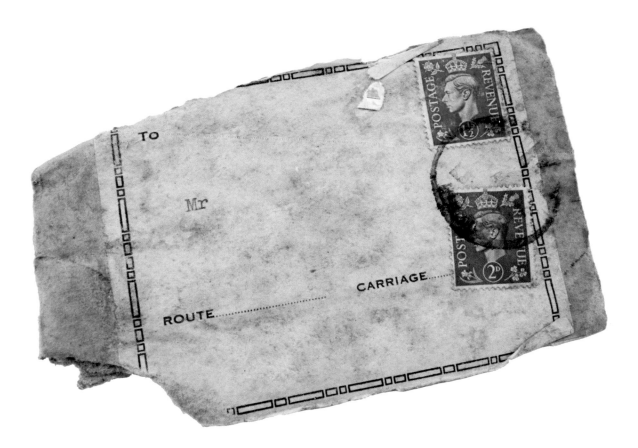

Despite the rights that accompanied the first postage stamps, some people still abused the system through counterfeiting. Once a stamped letter passed through the post office, the stamps were cancelled, crossed out with ink so that they couldn't be used again. Yet Hill and others in the postal service soon realized that the cancellation ink could easily be washed off without harming the stamp.

Hill immediately set up experiments to test new inks. Called the "rainbow trials," the tests helped him find inks less durable than the ones used for the Penny Black. He also held cancellation trials to rule out inks that could be easily removed without damaging the stamp. In February 1841, Hill introduced a replacement stamp, the "Penny Red," which would be used with stronger black cancellation ink. A less-durable ink for the Twopenny Blue was also introduced.

Stamp factory workers (opposite) had to work hard to keep up with the high demand for stamps.

Upon Rowland's retirement as postmaster general of Great Britain, Queen Victoria knighted him for his service to the country. A statue of him still stands across from the London Stock Exchange.

A fruity stamp from the northern African nation of Libya.

While Queen Victoria consented to the use of her image on the stamp, she never foresaw that it would spread around the globe. British stamps were immediately supplied to 60 British colonies and protectorates, and, in less than two decades, the idea launched by her simple portrait caught on in every country on every continent of the world. No matter if a country adorned its stamp with the face of a president, a famed animal of the region, or its most striking landscape, the stamp became a clear signal of identity—a way for a nation's citizens to know that there was a place to which they belonged.

Yet the boundaries of country and region would dissolve as the same scene replayed itself around the world. A mail carrier knocked on a door, slid letters through a mail slot, or piled mail into a post office box. The recipient, eyeing the stamp and the letter's origin, tore into the envelope and unfolded a long-awaited letter. While he or she read it, a voice came to life, as clear as if the person had been standing in the same room. Folding the letter back together, the recipient quietly stood for a moment, feeling the weighty breath of shared words in his or her hands.

In 1848, Irishman Henry Archer adapted a machine for perforating stamps, which allowed the perforation of 400,000 stamps per day. In 1854, the first perforated stamps were sold.

Stamps depicting images associated with Greece (above) and France (opposite).

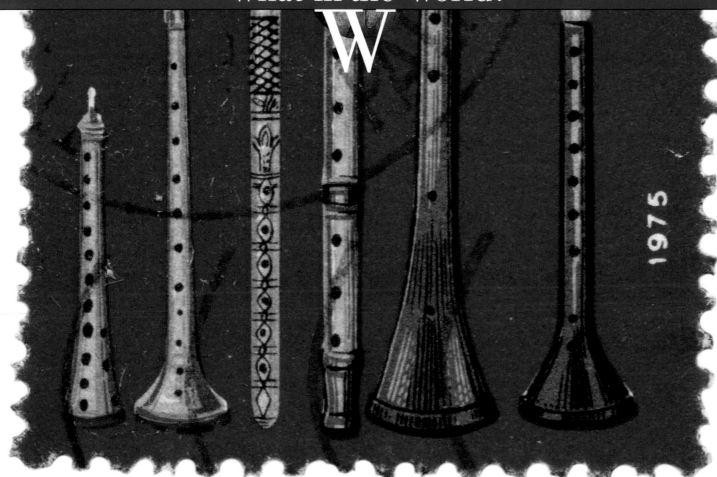

ΕΛΛΑΣ
HELLAS   ΔP. 11

W
What in the World?
W

1975

1795	Rowland Hill is born in Kidderminster, a small town in central England.
1798	British physician Edward Jenner announces his successful use of the smallpox vaccine.
1803	The Louisiana Purchase doubles the size of the U.S., expanding its western border to the Rocky Mountains.
1808	German composer Ludwig van Beethoven performs his Symphony no. 5 for the first time.
1812	Swiss traveler John Lewis Burckhardt discovers remains of the ancient Middle Eastern city of Petra.
1815	British citizens dance the quadrille, a square dance for four couples, for the first time.
1818	Scottish explorer John Ross searches the arctic for the Northwest Passage linking the Atlantic and Pacific oceans.
1821	The electric motor is invented by British chemist and physicist Michael Faraday.
1828	Shaka, the Zulu king and founder of the Zulu Nation in South Africa, is assassinated.
1831	French novelist Victor Hugo publishes *The Hunchback of Notre-Dame*, which would inspire a Gothic revival in architecture.
1840	The first stamp, the Penny Black, is introduced in England.
1853	Potato chips are invented in Saratoga Springs, New York, by chef George Crum.
1856	Fossils of prehistoric people are first discovered in Germany's Neanderthal valley.
1859	Construction of the Suez Canal begins in Egypt, connecting the Mediterranean and the Red seas.
1861–1865	The American Civil War is fought between the Union and the Confederacy.
1864	Rowland Hill is knighted for his contributions to Great Britain.
1866	The first Atlantic telegraph cable connects Great Britain and the U.S.
1869	Japan's first public elementary school opens in Kyoto.
1879	Upon his death, Sir Rowland Hill is buried at Westminster Abbey in London.

Copyright

Published by Creative Education
P.O. Box 227, Mankato, Minnesota 56002

Creative Education is an imprint of The Creative Company.
Design by Rita Marshall
Production design by The Design Lab

Photographs by Corbis (Academy of Natural Sciences of Philadelphia, The Art Archive, Bettmann, Blue Lantern Studio, Alexander Burkatovski, Christie's Images, Theodore Gerard, Hulton-Deutsch Collection, Jennifer Kennard, Charles & Josette Lenars, Araldo de Luca, Paper Rodeo, Reuters, Connie Ricca, Leonard de Selva), Getty Images (Hulton Archive, Time Life Pictures), iStockphoto

Illustration copyright © 1983 Jean-Louis Besson (page 15)

Library of Congress Cataloging-in-Publication Data
Fandel, Jennifer.
The postage stamp / by Jennifer Fandel.
p. cm. — (What in the world?)
Includes index.
ISBN-13: 978-1-58341-554-2
1. Postage stamps—Great Britain—History—Juvenile literature.
2. Postal service—Great Britain—History—Juvenile literature.
I. Title. II. Series.

HE6185.G7F36   2007   383.23—dc22   2006027450

First Edition
9 8 7 6 5 4 3 2 1

Index